Quotations, Sayings

and Words of

Wisdom of

Fr. James McDyer of

Glencolmcille

A special thanks to Margaret Cunningham and

Máire O'Gara at the Fr. James McDyer Folk Village,

Glencolmcille. Also, Mary Anne Gillespie for

photographs, Cath McGinley, Owen Lyons and others

too numerous to mention who helped in putting this

collection together for the 25th Anniversary of

Fr. McDyer's passing.

Liam Mc Ginley

Celebrating the 25th Anniversary of the Passing of Canon James McDyer

(1987 – 2012)

Knock as often at the half-door as you do at the brass knocker.

From: Original Booklet of Sayings

By Rev. J. Mc Dyer

Author's Note

It was always in my head that if I got the chance sometime I would put together a compilation of the best bits of Fr Mc Dyer's many colourful sayings and quotations. The inspiration for this came from a short collection prior to this one.

To the reader I admit that these may not all be the best of all his sayings, but, nevertheless, it is a fairly comprehensive selection and hopefully it will capture some of the character of the man. It is easy to see that he had a great flair for the effective sound bite, long before the term became popular in the modern press. His strong desire for exact descriptions and spiritual meaning seems to have sustained him through much adversity and difficult times.

As the quotations tend to show, there was a huge anxiety in the man to try and help the people of Glencolmcille and in doing so help the church renew itself. He was very aware of the power of words and wanted to be a radical in a time of change.

The preservation of the Irish race was another big concern of his but now seems a farfetched dream when Irish material sovereignty, so important and so hard fought for in 1916, has been given away to Europe without a challenge.

I hope that this selection gives some enjoyment to the reader. In these darkened times, it is hard to find solace, but Fr Mc Dyer's words are a powerful reminder that anyone can make a difference.

Liam Mc Ginley, 3rd June 2012

The problems of West Donegal are not new in origin. In a sense, some of the causes of the problems have been present since the passing of the Ice-Age.

A Report written in 1970
By Fr. James McDyer

Each village should aim at a target of 3 industries with a minimum of 200 employed.

A Report written in 1970
By Fr. James McDyer

I feel that there is great
hope for West Donegal. Out
of adversity there is often
born steely determination,
great hardihood and great
success.

From: 'West Donegal Resource Survey,
an appraisal
By Rev. J. Mc Dyer

I suppose the number of parishes in Ireland - indeed the world – that can claim to have six ancient pilgrimages, are very rare and it is a tribute to the asceticism and the depth of the peoples' faith that they have lasted so long.

A Guide to Glencolmcille
By Fr. James McDyer 12/7/1974

What we want is quick thinking, clear thinking, courageous thinking, and big thinking. The day is gone when we can afford the luxury of dilly dallying. The words "Ní féidir" and "Is cuma liom" should be heard less and less. They should be replaced by "Un tosaigh".

West Donegal Resource Survey

- An appraisal

By Rev. J. McDyer, October 1970

The land alone will never save Glencolmcille. Neither will the weaving factory. Not even together could they do it. What we needed was four or five pillars on which to build.

From: The Importance of Being Irish,
By Alan Bestic, 1968
Fr. James Mc Dyer

Before I came here I worked in London. I met a lot of emigrants there, mostly from rural areas, and the sight of them made me feel a sort of shame, that we had to depend on a country we had fought, to absorb our redundant youth. We seemed to be getting priorities wrong – talking about the past and doing nothing about the present. Going on about self-discipline and efficiency being the price of freedom, but not paying the price.

Fr. James Mc Dyer
From: The Importance of Being Irish,
By Alan Bestic, 1968

Being a farmer's son, my first concern was for the proper utilization of the land. Aware of the innate skills of the local people, I aimed that the Show should stimulate pride in farming achievement, needlework and home baking.
Our council and several others worked with might and main to make it a success.

An Autobiography,
Fr. James McDyer 1982

Port is remarkable as an example of a deserted village. The gurgling stream, the pretty bridge, the little green paddocks, the gleaming Cladagh, and the frowning hills which forever stand guard against the raging sea, all conspire to make this haven by the sea a place of unsurpassed beauty and peace.

A Guide to Glencolmcille, (Port)
By Rev. J. McDyer 12/7/1974

What I would like to see is an agricultural college in each homogeneous region with two or three parishes as the catchment area, where the students would commute whilst residing on their father's farm and wherein the principles of co-operation and the very latest methods of husbandry suitable to their particular region would be taught.

Article by Rev. J. McDyer 1/5/1970
The Democrat, Supplement

St Conall died at his monastery in Inniskeel Island near Narin in 596. He was both a cousin and a contemporary of St Colmcille. Indeed, legend claims that the two Saints had a meeting place near the top of Glengesh Pass where they often met and conferred.

A Guide to Glencolmcille
By Rev. J. McDyer 12/7/1974

In your encounter with the local people on all these Social Evenings, you may find them slightly reserved at first, but this is due to innate courtesy by which they think it indelicate to intrude, but as you get to know them a little better you will discover a deep friendliness within them and you can, if you wish, have the pleasure of conversing with them in two languages.

Guide to Glencolmcille
By Rev. J. McDyer 12/7/1974

There is probably a signpost here to Maghery. Three or four miles along this road and you come to an enchanted world. On your left is the waterfall which drops so far and so perpendicular that it looks suspended in the air like a swathe of finest lace.

A Guide to Glencolmcille
By Rev. J. McDyer 12/7/1974

From my own experience with the farming community, it would seem to me that the two greatest causes of their malaise are lack of capital and lack of education.... But I do say that it should not be beyond the capacity of government to take more drastic measures, so that Irish money should be made fight for Ireland.

Article by Rev. J. McDyer 1/5/1970
The Democrat, Supplement

Few people up here had heard of celery. The Department of Agriculture had heard of it, all right, but they said we wouldn't be able to grow it here. They spent a couple of hours pleading with me not to grow vegetables, saying it was too stormy, too dark, too everything. But I started and they grew beautifully. They suit the pocket handkerchiefs of land we have here.

From: The Importance of Being Irish,
by Alan Bestic, 1968
Fr. James Mc Dyer

The debate between Willie Cunningham and O'Boyle was fast and furious. Both languages – Irish and English were used and though I could not follow all the nuances of the Irish language, I know that several holy names were invoked and I don't think they were invoked in prayer... On the following morning I again visited the O' Boyle family and amazingly I found them willing to talk business.

Fr. James McDyer, from his article in 1984, The Founding of Pairc na nGael, in the Naomh Columba GAA Historical Magazine

Turn to the left up the beautiful Greannie Glen. When you come to the top, switch off your engine and look back. The sight is truly inspiring the vast tunnel of the Glen; the little village set in the midst of green sward; the golden sands of the sea beyond.

A Guide to Glencolmcille
By Rev. J. McDyer 12/7/1974

Soil is a living thing and it will drown if not drained. Soil is vibrant with life and it will starve if not fed. Control of weeds and control of pests has made fantastic advances since the advent of the humble spraying-machine.

From: 'West Donegal Resource Survey
An appraisal by Rev. J. Mc Dyer

Surely it is not beyond the competence of the West Donegal people, either working through local committees or through one general committee to institute such an industrial drive.

From: 'West Donegal Resource Survey
An appraisal by Rev. J. Mc Dyer

It has long been said, rightly or wrongly, that the women of Donegal by their diligence in producing such Home-Crafts as knitting, crochet and embroidery, have kept our economy from total collapse.

From: 'West Donegal Resource Survey
An appraisal by Rev. J. Mc Dyer

"Before us is the magnificent Parish Hall, executed with such speed, finished with such skill, and erected by the wholehearted co-operation of the people of Glencolmcille, Catholic and Protestant alike."

Donegal Democrat
Fr. J McDyer, 10th April 1953

The real antagonists of the co-operatives were always those who tried to monopolise and exploit for their own private gain.

The teachings of Christ favour co-operation and socialism and His enemies were those who were abusing power.

An Autobiography,
Fr. James McDyer 1982

It is no exaggeration to say that it is among Ireland's most beautiful valleys; and it certainly is one of the more secluded. The scenery is breath-taking, whether it is the Glen itself ringed on three sides by mountains, and opening onto a sandy beach and the sea, or the houses of the glen as they clutch precariously to its hillsides.

An Autobiography,
Fr. James McDyer 1982

Two theories exist about the origin of these stones.

The first theory is that they were the marking stones which designated the boundaries of Monastic lands.

The second theory, which is the more widely accepted, claims that these originated from the Megalithic period and were possible objects of pagan reverence.

Guide to Glencolmcille
By Rev. J. McDyer 12/7/1974

Do not say that you
love your country
because she is great.
Rather let us show
that she is great
because of the
patriotism and the
unity of her children.

From: Original Booklet of Sayings
By Rev. J. Mc Dyer

"We are unfortunate that we have a regime in this Republic which has become so reliant for progress on State-sponsored projects and foreign industrialists that it tends to view with supercilious scorn the efforts of a purely native community project."

Fr. J. McDyer's speech to a visiting delegation of 33 international professors and lecturers to Glencolmcille on 12th of July 1964, reported in Donegal Democrat.

If these conditions go unchecked, they will reduce to poverty a large proportion of those now engaged in agriculture and commerce; they will disrupt a society which withstood adversity for centuries and they will blot out for ever much that is finest in Irish heritage...

It is the purpose of the Defence of the West to sound a note of alarm which will be heard and heeded. It is their purpose to urge for better production and to continue to keep asking for adequate capital.

Fr. James Mc Dyer, Save *the West,* The Emerald Hall, Hammersmith, London, 1/5/1966.
Chairman: Fr. Eamonn Casey.

I believe that if a thing is right and good, you should not surrender because of obstacles. I may or may not be right, but if your cause is good and just then, if you come to a brick wall, you should either get over it or go through it.

From: Original Booklet of Sayings
By Rev. J. Mc Dyer

The monuments have not remained aloof, unrelated to the people of the Glen.
They are part of a living tradition, and the well-trodden paths around many a cairn or standing stone are silent testimony that here the present has always met the past. In this, Glencolmcille perhaps is unique.

Fr. James McDyer's preface to Michael Herrity's book
Glencolmcille, A Guide to 5,000 Years
History in Stone, 1971

About one mile above the little circular Church of Burt you can visit the famous Grianach of Aileach with its remarkable legend of the sleeping horsemen who await the final battle for the freedom of Ireland.

Guide to Glencolmcille
By Rev. J. McDyer 12/7/1974

At Malin Head you will stand at the most northerly point in Ireland and if the day is clear and you look North-Eastward you will see the Hebrides rising from the distant sea.

Guide to Glencolmcille
By Rev. J. McDyer 12/7/1974

I always claimed that our religious duty was not fully executed if it was a vertical religion in the form of joining our hands praying to God. It also had to be horizontal in the sense that you stretched out to other people and from that point of view, well, it was an extension of my work as a priest.

Fr. James McDyer interview on RTE Radio with Kevin O' Kelly in 1982

As you climb up the steep Mill Brae
there is, across the stream on your left -
but it remains not seen from the road
the remains of yet another little monastic
foundation dating from the early
centuries and called "Teampall na
Manach."which is literally the Church of
the Monks. It is a small building with what
appears to be gravestones close by. I
know of no record of its date but it
would seem to be very old.

Guide to Glencolmcille
By Rev. J. McDyer 12/7/1974

Defeatists say it is too late, that too few people remain in the West to promote a struggle, that indifference to the social and additional issues involved in the fate of the West is too widespread. This we deny.

Fr. James Mc Dyer, *Save the West,* The Emerald Hall, Hammersmith, London, 1/5/1966. Chairman: Fr. Eamonn Casey.

Let us attack the problems of our country with vigour, with determination, in a spirit of dedication and with unity and in charity.
Let us toil that our country will bloom with prosperity. Let us so work that our individuality will be preserved in language, in dancing and in games.
Let us so act that a spirit of Christian charity will glow from the very soul of Ireland.
Thus, and only thus, can we effectively pay tribute to our patriot dead. So will visions be made into realities and visions become of sterner stuff.

Fr Mc Dyer's speech at the Scallan
1916 Golden Jubilee Celebration in April 1966

However, I felt that I could not carry out my spiritual ministry and ignore the social and economic plight of my people. To be indifferent to this would run contrary to the virtues of justice and charity.

A Report written in 1970
By Fr. James McDyer

I had no illusions about the awesome task confronting us in Glencolmcille. Its remoteness, its poor resources, the erosion of the flower of youth through emigration; the psychological effects of the administration of the Dole and the frugal security it offered.

A Report written in 1970
By Fr. James McDyer

So great was the fame of
Naomh Aodh macBricne, or
Saint Hugh, and so prestigious
was the Turas which had been
perpetuated in his memory, that
Sliabh a Liag ranked with
Mount Brandon in Kerry and
Croagh Patrick in Mayo as one
of the three holy mountains of
Ireland.

Guide to Glencolmcille
By Rev. J. McDyer 12/7/1974

Indeed, in the course of the succeeding years, the profits of the Hall were used to help many of our projects in social development.

In this way people were provided with entertainment and in availing of it they were helping their community.

A Report written in 1970
By Fr. James McDyer

For instance, my very first effort was to have a Glass Farm which would carry three crops per year and which would run side by side with a large central Piggery and Poultry Farm. This was duly surveyed and approved, but for reasons best known to the Minister for Agriculture he would not give me a loan or a grant.

A Report written in 1970
By Fr. James McDyer

Our policy is that the sources of wealth in Glencolmcille should be owned by the people of Glencolmcille. In helping to exploit these resources, we will welcome the marketing capabilities, the expertise and a proportion of capital of any firm whether it be State sponsored or private.

Fr. James McDyer at the AGM
of the Machine-Knitting Factory in 1968

Let us not cease our sacrifices and endeavours until the agony of emigration, the pinch of penury and the slur of indolence shall have been lifted from the brows of men.

From: Original Booklet of Sayings
By Rev. J. Mc Dyer (1966)

The difference between our Co-Operative and Private Enterprise is that we are not working for ourselves: we are working to develop the potential of the district and keep
our own people at home.

Guide to Glencolmcille
By Rev. J. McDyer 12/7/1974

As a priest I would not take part in party politics because I viewed them as divisive. As an individual I regarded the main parties as opportunist.

Looking back, I am now sorry that I did not agree to organise a march on Dublin from the West of Ireland.

An Autobiography
By Fr. James McDyer of Glencolmcille

That's one of the troubles about the west. It was the progressive ones who left. Anyway, to get back, I knew roads and water and electric light were not enough.

From: The Importance of Being Irish,
By Alan Bestic, 1968
Fr. James Mc Dyer

None of it made any sense as long as there still were twenty five young people leaving Glencolmcille each year. I knew I had to provide work, an incentive; and that was when I began thinking of co-operatives.

From: The Importance of Being Irish,
By Alan Bestic, 1968
Fr. James Mc Dyer

Can they generate sufficient cohesion and drive to focus the attention of Government on the need for capital investment in their community?

Are they in this year of 1965 prepared to cry halt to the sources of dereliction and dispersal? If the answer is no, then we will progressively deteriorate as communities until we are too weak to recuperate.

Fr. James Mc Dyer
From: The Donegal Democrat,
1st January 1965

One of the highest summits to which the human being might soar was the practical love and help of his neighbour, for God's sake, and one of the lowest depths to which the able-bodied and healthy might descend was to become dependent on others for his keep.

Fr. James McDyer, Irish Independent,
26/5/1964

I always maintained that the time was coming that wild fish would become so scarce that people would be forced into mariculture and aquaculture just as their ancestors, eight thousand years ago were forced to abandon the hunting of wild animals and concentrate on agriculture instead.

An Autobiography,
Fr. James McDyer 1982

I have always been sustained by the
motto of the late Canon Hayes
which was- "Better to light a candle
than to forever curse the darkness".
My motto was more radical – "Better
to light ten candles even though
nine of them are extinguished".

An Autobiography,
Fr. James McDyer 1982

Perhaps, I was driving too hard to turn the community into a family that was my ideal, which I did not achieve. But still in all, they are definitely an identifiable close knit community. That is a fact not my doing."

Fr. James McDyer in a 1981 interview
with Kevin O' Kelly, RTE Radio

But if the time comes when more and more merging of small holdings in bigger units, with a consequent diminishing of population on the soil, reaches its logical conclusion – no statistics can mask the collapse of worthwhile Irish economy.

Fr. James McDyer
Publication Vexilla Regis in 1966

The stone walls around the tiny fields look deceptively timeless – but they are in fact, a relatively recent feature. The ancient system of 'Rundale', where unfenced land was allocated in strips and plots and the tradition of 'booleying' (where families and cattle moved seasonally between islands, inshore and hills) still survived in some parts of Donegal up to the present century.

Fr. James McDyer,
Irish Independent 8/12/1973

I was dissuaded from bee-farming because, although there was plenty of heather, there was too little clover. Noting the enormous amount of furze or whins, I sent off samples to be examined for perfume content, but this was too low to justify the manufacture of perfume.
Even the making of chalk for sale to Irish schools was suggested, this time by an English well-wisher, but the Institute of Industrial Research and Standards advised me that the market was too limited to justify the cost of capitalization.

An Autobiography,
Fr. James McDyer 1982

We of the Errigal Co-Operative Society are grateful to you all - public representatives and people from many walks of life for coming here today, and we are particularly grateful to Mr. Lemass for gracing the occasion with his presence. For by doing so he has set the seal of approval and encouragement on the project we have launched.

Fr. James McDyer,
Donegal Democrat, 14/12/1962

They forget that there are many men and women left in Ireland yet both in public life and in private organisation who are inspired by the loftiest motives of patriotism. Those ideals can be carried out no matter what the obstacles, if they are flanked by the grim determination we have got in the Errigal Co-Operative and our watch word is; Come what may, under God we will come through.

Fr. James McDyer,
Donegal Democrat, 14/12/1962

First I took advice from the Agriculture Institute to keep me on the right lines. I showed them my plans and they gave them the green light, economically. After that I approached 130 local farmers and said: Folks, how about knocking those fences down and working as one family? I guarantee three basics to every house: free turf for your fire; potatoes and milk; and work at standard agricultural rates for every able-bodied man in the community.

Fr. James Mc Dyer
From: The Importance of Being Irish,
By Alan Bestic, 1968

I suppose I could solve the whole problem by the stroke of a pen, by luring in one big enterprise to run the lot. But I believe that God gave us land for a purpose; and it's wrong to denude that land.

Fr. James Mc Dyer
From: The Importance of Being Irish,
By Alan Bestic, 1968

I'm sufficient of a socialist to feel that it would not be fair to bring a big capitalist here to cream off the profit, pay the serfs, perhaps, at the first sigh of recession, pull out, leaving everyone high and dry.

Fr. James Mc Dyer
From: The Importance of Being Irish,
By Alan Bestic, 1968

"Soon the flags will be lowered, the drums will be muted and the speeches will be curtailed. This does not mean that the memory of their deeds will be erased from our minds. Our greatest tribute can be in the manner in which we carry ourselves for the next fifty years. We are not to die for Ireland: we are to live for Ireland. Let us so comfort ourselves that these following years will become golden years in Irish history."

Fr Mc Dyer's speech at the Scallan as reported in the Donegal Democrat,
1916 Golden Jubilee Celebration in April 1966

Let us attack the problems of
our country with vigour and
determination, in a spirit of
dedication, with unity and
charity.

Fr Mc Dyer's speech at the Scallan
1916 Golden Jubilee Celebration in April 1966

It is not our purpose today to extol
their heroic martyrdom – their deeds
have spoken louder than words, but
it is our duty to remember them with
awe, with admiration and in prayer.

Fr Mc Dyer's speech at the Scallan
1916 Golden Jubilee Celebration in April 1966

"We, and our contemporaries, can be likened to a vast Pilgrimage of people, who are traversing across life to the destination of eternity, we are in this together and it is incumbent on those who are surging ahead whether spiritually or materially to reach back their hands and help those who are flagging to fall back in line."

Fr. James McDyer's booklet
The Island of the Setting Sun

Patrick Mc Gill was almost certainly disappointed in the reaction of his fellow countrymen to his criticism of the parish priest, but he underestimated the extremely deep respect of the Irish people for their pastor, however autocratic he might be. Neither did he realise that many Irish people would have felt betrayed by such an attack, for to them Catholicism and Nationalism were intertwined.

From a Lecture given by Fr. James McDyer at the
Patrick McGill Festival, Glenties,
6th September 1982.

In prose and poetry Patrick McGill trod the path of many world-famous writers before him, but in applying the microscope to the social injustice of his experience, he was a man before his time and a pioneer and skilled observer in unmasking the brutishness of life which was the lot of the working class in these islands.

From a Lecture given by Fr. James McDyer at the Patrick McGill Festival, Glenties, 6th September 1982.

"And fair play to the people of Glencolmcille, a hundred and ten of them were agreeable to communise for ten years... That was the great might have been and the tragedy of tragedies that the responsible department in Dublin hadn't the sagacity or the nerve to support that, which was supported by some departments in Dublin. We would have either have failed or we would have succeeded. If we had failed it wasn't a terrible loss – it was experimental work, but if we had succeeded as I'm fairly convinced we would, then we had created a tremendous headline for the small farm areas of rural Ireland."

Fr. James McDyer Interview
with Kevin O"Kelly on RTE Radio, in 1980.

I did the stimulating verbally in the Church, in announcements, in small school meetings, even kitchen meetings. But I began to discover that the verbal relationship that I had with them was not quite getting through, they didn't realise properly that they had **a revolution on their hands.**"

Fr McDyer said in an interview with Kevin O'
Kelly in Glencolmcille
for RTE in 1981

Let the message go out
from Glencolmcille to
the underdeveloped
parishes of the country
that it is time the policy
of Help Yourself was
overwhelmed by the
policy of Self Help.

Fr. James McDyer, Donegal Democrat,
23/8/1968

I yearn now for a world war of a different kind. Not the projected nuclear war, but a war against the claims of nations to territories which are not their own.

An Autobiography,
Fr. James McDyer 1982

If there is a spark of civilization beneath the veneer, this is the world war which should be fought, and fought with the billions that are now being squandered on instruments of destruction.

An Autobiography,
Fr. James McDyer 1982

It was certainly not my strategy to dissipate my energies by travelling hither and thither to address meetings, but I disliked refusing and so, over a period of six or seven years, I reckon that I addressed meetings in thirty out of the thirty two counties of Ireland, and also some in Britain, Holland and France.

An Autobiography,
Fr. James McDyer 1982

The two principal political parties in the Republic avidly espoused the cause of entry to the EEC. They were joyously joined by the large farmers and a considerable segment of the Civil Service.

An Autobiography,
Fr. James McDyer 1982

Naturally, I was worried about the fate of the small farmers, and I also wondered whether there would be a stampede of foreign capital as had been envisaged.

An Autobiography,
Fr. James McDyer 1982

The agony of abject poverty must be lifted from the brows of men, we must turn our eyes outward to the 600 to 800 million of our fellow humans in this global village and adopt them, community by community.

From a Lecture given by Fr. James McDyer at the Patrick McGill Festival, Glenties, 6th September 1982.

The priest could act as a welding force to heal the breaches and join the conflicting loyalties within the community. He could also inspire people to greater civic spirit and to greater efficiency and hard work.

Fr. James McDyer, Irish Independent, 16/11/1967

Any attempt at solving the problems of rural Ireland in merely economic terms denuded the rural areas of their people. This disappearance of rural people would result in a loss of many of the virtues and values which made our whole country such a Christian force in the world.

Fr. James McDyer, Irish Independent, 16/11/1967

We are deeply grateful to all those people who helped, whether they be from Glencolmcille or city based industries, the Government Departments who helped us with licenses and grants, and the many people overseas why by their sympathy and practical help gave Glencolmcille the encouragement we needed.

Fr. James McDyer,
Donegal Democrat, 23/8/1968

We would like to see the 'buy Irish' campaign gather momentum and strength. We would like to see Ireland move into the '70s with a new concept of patriotism – not the patriotism of the public platform or the battle field, but the patriotism and the skill of the Irish salesmen abroad, backed by the hard work and efficiency of the Irish labourers at home; a patriotism which will not have complete political freedom as its immediate goal, but will first and foremost aim at complete economic independence which has eluded us for so long.

Fr. James McDyer,
Donegal Democrat, December 1968

Donegal was one of the three major tourism areas in the country, and although its gross receipts on tourism reached £8.7 million per annum, if it was properly organised from within and without, it could double and even treble that figure. When the gross national take was 78 million, it was easy to see why Donegal was playing a major role.

Fr. James McDyer's speech at Irish Hotels Federation meeting reported in Donegal Democrat on 12/5/1967

The developed nations are doing something to meet the challenge of world poverty, illiteracy and disease, but their efforts fall so far short of their potential that nothing less than a revolution in their thinking and their policy will bring about what is really needed.

Fr. James McDyer said in his preface to the 1965 book: *The Last Revolution*, by L. J. Lebret

The Industrial Parade we have witnessed here today may not be by city standards very impressive, but as a parade in a remote, rural district like Glencolmcille it has an inspiring message for us.

Fr. James McDyer, Donegal Democrat 23/8/1968

It is true that your products are enthusiastically bought by some of the most high class stores in America and Canada, but they are not bought because the products are from Glencolmcille or even because they are from Ireland. They are bought because they are top quality.

Fr. James McDyer, Donegal Democrat 13/12/1968

The development had yet to be done. The field had been serrated by ridges in the agricultural use of previous years. Sean O'hIghne and Willie Cunningham and I persuaded the Parish Council to plant a crop of potatoes in the field and then sow grass-seed in it. This was willingly done because all of us in the Parish Council required a good spacious field for the Glencolmcille Shows.

Fr. James McDyer, article, The Founding of Pairc na nGael in the 1964 Naomh Columba GAA magazine.

At this time I also had a very socialist dream which, unfortunately, was to remain a dream. In a low resource area such as ours I felt that the profits of any enterprise should be owned by the people, and utilized for the good of the people. If they were scooped up by the owners of private enterprises the people of the locality would never attain any status greater than wage-earners.

An Autobiography,
Fr. James McDyer 1982

The Political parties of
Ireland have turned the
land into a battlefield
where self-interest takes
priority over party and
party takes priority over the
common good. If anything
is for the common good let
not cynicism, criticism or
frustration stop us on our
way.

From: Original Booklet of Sayings
By Rev. J. McDyer

We in the Errigal Co-operative are inspired to love of land, and we like to think we are arisen in a new Rebellion. Our rising is against the forces of apathy, decay, and despair of the countryside."

Fr Mc Dyer's Speech at Errigal's 1st Year's AGM

"

But having started this great work I hope they will have it duplicated a hundred times, because our oft-repeated statement in the Errigal Co-operative is that if it can be done here, it can be done anywhere."

Fr. James McDyer speaking at opening of The
Errigal Factory
10th December 1962

It should not be forgotten that many of the underdeveloped nations of the West have their own underdeveloped areas. Let them first gain experience of practical Christianity and let them first show example by putting their regions of poverty in order and let them overwhelm the barriers of greed and transcend the temptations of political patronage and expediency.

Fr. James McDyer said in his preface to the 1965 book:
The Last Revolution, by L. J. Lebret

"They say Mac, you have a mystique – I tell them there is no mystique, it's just as I always say, give me the man any day, who's prepared to make nine mistakes and one success, instead of the lad who'll sit forever in his chair, cursing the darkness."

From the Book, *On Our Knees* by Rosita Sweetman, Ireland 1972.

Electricity was the next big thing. Before I came the elders of the village had met and decided against having electricity because it was too dear and too dangerous! Well I had to combat that, and then go and make a nuisance of myself in the County Council.

From the Book, *On Our Knees* by Rosita Sweetman, Ireland 1972.

Those few of us who are deeply involved would endure and do the same again and more, not only for the sheer delight of meeting and overcoming problems with accomplishments but also because we believe that we are trying to fulfil the other half of our religion.

Guide to Glencolmcille
By Rev. J. McDyer 12/7/1974

I have tried to point out to you some of the riches of Glencolmcille.
In doing so, I am confident that your visit to Glencolmcille will have been made more interesting and, I hope more pleasant.

Guide to Glencolmcille
By Rev. J. McDyer 12/7/1974

"There is a need for a reappraisal of the whole Christian message of the West. The teaching of the pulpits must be translated more vigorously into action. 'Love your Neighbour' must not merely be a matter of assent, but it must be expressed in deed."

Fr. James McDyer said in his preface to the 1965 book: The Last Revolution, by L. S. Lebret

There is a famine abroad in our land. It is not the famine of gold or silver or bread. But it is a famine of great men and women. The world today is suffering from a great nemesis of mediocrity. We are dying from ordinariness; we are perishing from pettiness.

From a Lecture given by Fr. James McDyer at the Patrick McGill Festival, Glenties, 6th September 1982.

Strange as it may seem, the standard of living attained by the employed and the unemployed in our day compared to the era of Patrick McGill, is now so high that in the past few years there is a grave danger that we may have passed the barrier which the State and Industry can economically afford

From a Lecture given by Fr. James McDyer at the Patrick McGill Festival, Glenties, 6th September 1982.

Before me there is the rotation montage of my experiences down the arches of the ages – the fight for Irish freedom; the polyphony of the Maynooth choir; the day of ordination; the bombed rubble of the London streets; the isolation of Tory island; the effortless gliding of a seabird over the cliffs of Sliabh Liag.; the eager faces of audiences in many parts as they waited for a message of hope; the sleepless nights of worry; the inimitable friendliness of the Irish people. And when the kaleidoscope of memories is stilled, I say to myself, "Glencolmcille, I would walk your fields again".

An Autobiography,
Fr. James McDyer 1982

If one-quarter of the human race continues to reside in an ivory tower and surrounds itself by more wealth and comfort and patronisingly allows the unwanted crumbs to fall to the poor, then the day of reckoning will surely come. And their now seemingly impregnable position will be first eroded and eventually overrun by the agonised and out-raged three quarters of humanity.

Fr. James McDyer said in his preface to the 1965 book: The Last Revolution, by L. J. Lebret

And so, I salute Patrick McGill as a courageous pioneer; as a distinguished writer; and as a man whose compassion for those who are wronged led him to attack those who wronged them.

As a fellow-Glenties man, I salute him across the span of one generation to another.

From a Lecture given by Fr. James McDyer at the Patrick McGill Festival, Glenties, 6th September 1982.

Our Country, after living in the back-wash for many years, is now at least struggling to its feet. Soon we may be thrown into a grinding struggle for survival in competition with other nations. In that struggle we may go under, if our country boys and girls continue to set their sights on horizons far away, and we continue to export to other nations, the education that is gleaned and the talent that is developed in our national schools.

Fr. James McDyer,
Donegal Democrat, 28/9/1962

I like to look on a school in a larger context. I like to think of it as a Co-operative in which teachers, children, parents, managers and inspectors, play a vital role and the close co-ordination of their efforts should bring about a most satisfactory result.

Fr. James McDyer,
Donegal Democrat, 28/9/1962

In the second place, I'm sufficient of a socialist to feel that it would not be fair to bring a big capitalist here to cream off the profit, pay the serfs and then, perhaps, at the first sign of recession, pull out, leaving everyone high and dry.
To my way of thinking, all sources of wealth in Glencolmcille belong to the people of Glencolmcille; and the frontiers of the family are not the four walls of the house anymore, but the perimeter of the community in which they live.

From: The Importance of Being Irish,
By Alan Bestic, 1968

"I think if you can't develop the local resources of the area then you can forget about it. The second thing was, not to be sitting around debating about getting someone in with a big industrial base behind him – you'd be pushing up daisies before any of them arrived."

From the Book, *On Our Knees* by Rosita Sweetman, Ireland 1972.

Let the message go out from Glencolmcille to the underdeveloped parishes of the country that it is time the policy of Help Yourself was overwhelmed by the policy of Self Help.

Fr. James McDyer, Donegal Democrat, 23/8/1968

Yes! It was Sean O'hIghne and Willie Cunningham, and I knew at once they had something important to discuss, I was wrong! It was not something important! It was something very momentous! From our conversation and decision there emerged the birth of the Gaelic Park in Glencolmcille.

Fr Mc Dyer, The Founding of Pairc na nGael.
Naomh Columba GAA Magazine 1984

"My original objection to a community becoming totally dependent on the State and the good will of politicians and bureaucrats was now augmented by a new objection, and this was that no community should become dependent on the good will of private enterprise. I was conscious that I was travelling along the road towards radical socialism."

An Autobiography,
Fr. James McDyer 1982

I hope that in the years to come they will concentrate their efforts not only on Gaelic Football but on the promotion of all kinds of athletics. May their efforts be crowned with success in the coming years and the sounds of acclamation resound throughout the Glen.

Fr. James McDyer, article, The Founding of Pairc na nGael in the 1964 Naomh Columba GAA magazine.

We have become so concerned with the creation of the sinews of war to enforce peace, that we now overlook the more obvious solution of the creation of the sinews of peace which is the fulfilment of the yearnings of the poor everywhere.. We are bemused by our initial achievements in reaching for other planets. Yet, it would seem much more important for us to grapple effectively with the problems of productivity, poverty and disease on earth before we reach beyond.

Fr. James McDyer said in his preface to the 1965 book:
The Last Revolution, by L. J. Lebret

At this time I also had a very socialist dream which, unfortunately, was to remain a dream. In a low resource area such as ours I felt that the profits of any enterprise should be owned by the people, and utilized for the good of the people. If they were scooped up by the owners of private enterprises the people of the locality would never attain any status greater than wage-earners.

An Autobiography,
Fr. James McDyer 1982

Ever since the young men of Glencolmcille had first begun to play Gaelic Football, they never had a field but had to make do with the local strand as a playing pitch, inserting goal posts for each match, using hemp-rope as cross-bars, and timing their encounters with the ebb and flow of the tide.

Fr Mc Dyer, The Founding of Pairc na nGael. GAA Magazine 1984, 1st Year's AGM

I was sick listening to the talk of politicians saying what they were going to do for the area, so in my innocence I wrote to Dev. Just to make sure he got the message I wrote to his wife Sinead, as well. I think I met the man once. Well it worked. Within three months we had our factory.

From the Book, *On Our Knees* by Rosita Sweetman, Ireland 1972.

"There is a need for a reappraisal of the whole Christian message of the West. The teaching of the pulpits must be translated more vigorously into action. 'Love your Neighbour' must not merely be a matter of assent, but it must be expressed in deed."

Fr. James McDyer said in his preface to the 1965
book: The Last Revolution,
by L. S. Lebret

"Never before was it so necessary to emphasise the solidarity of the human race. Never before was it so necessary to stress the worldwide brotherhood and family under one Father. Never before was it so necessary for the more affluent members of the human family to come to the aid of the poorer and to do so with careful international planning and with love."

Fr. James McDyer said in his preface to the 1965 book: *The Last Revolution*, by L. S. Lebret

All over the world there are billions of pounds spent annually in the manufacture of weapons of destruction, and a sizeable proportion of the most competent people in the world are engaged therein. What is the reason that supposedly civilized humankind should be engaged in this foolishness?

An Autobiography,
Fr. James McDyer 1982

Canon James Mc Dyer in Conversation with Kevin O Kelly in 1981 by permission of RTE.

I met Canon James McDyer by lucky chance two weeks ago where he and I were both speaking at a Historical Society meeting in Trinity University College. There was a suitably provocative subject for debate "the role of the Catholic Church in Irish life" and in this context it struck me that Canon McDyer was speaking much more in hope than in celebration.

He was, to be sure, eloquent about a vision for the younger generation of priests here in Ireland – he wanted them to encourage their people to help themselves out of the trough of despondency, to get up and go and not wait for outsiders to take initiatives. Certainly, his vision of priesthood, or ministry extended far outside the precincts of the Church and the administration of the sacraments, like himself, he wanted the young priest to be with their people inside and outside their purely religious concerns.

In fact, I think that he would have denied any obvious boundary between worldly and otherworldly ambitions. He spoke just a few days ago now, not like a man who had accomplished much but rather like one who had left much undone. It was obvious that he was modest about his own achievements. He obviously felt that he had miles to go and promises to keep and it was the same when I spoke to him up in Carrick, County Donegal on a bitter cold winter evening seven years ago.

We sat by the fire and he looked over what had been done and left undone.

Fr James Mc Dyer:
I started off life in Glencolmcille with the idea that here was a dying community, lovely people, very very nice, quiet and to a certain extent they had worked out a .... you wouldn't call it a culture of their own but a way of life of their own.

The community was really dying because of massive emigration, which had always been a way of life there, but in the early 50s when I came to Glencolmcille, emigration had taken a pernicious turn. So, I considered that it was, perhaps an extension of the priest's work to try and stem this emigration and create job opportunities for the people.

Just by that, some of the older conservative priests of the time might think that I was stepping outside the mould of a country priest. Perhaps, I was to a certain extent, but I make no apologies for it – I favour the Ten Commandments: God only had three Commandments that related to Himself and he had a whole whacken big seven of them that related to other people. Consequently, as a Christian, a Catholic and a priest, I always claimed that our religious duty was not fully executed if it was a vertical religion only, in the form of joining your hands, praying to god. It also, had to be horizontal, in the sense that you stretched out to other people. From that point of view, well it was an extension of my work as a priest all right – I admit that top priority is the generation of the spiritual atmosphere in the people under your care, that's top priority in a priest's work.

But the other one, I put it a second to that (very close to it in importance), well, the Gospel, all the Scriptures, particularly in the New Testament emphasises that point.

So, my first concern, when I arrived in Glencolmcille was to extend the duties of a priest there, and raise my voice not just in protest but also raise my voice to stimulate the people to try and help themselves.

Kevin O'Kelly:
It has been suggested that though your voice was a very powerful one, one that was heard as far away as Dublin by Eamonn de Valera among other people and I remember that you had considerable help from him and Mrs de Valera. Still the people of Glencolmcille, in the heel of the hunt, only a handful of them, it has been suggested really listened, and only a handful answered your call?

Fr James Mc Dyer:
To a large extent that is true, but however to say that it is fully true wouldn't be fair to the people of Glencolmcille. For instance, one of the first chores, to build a community hall and I sent out the word to the people of Glencolmcille that we would all have to co-operate on the building of the community hall. Every day, I would have thirty volunteers and the hall was built by voluntary labour. All we had to pay for were the bricks, mortar and timber. I intended it to be a massive first step in co-operation and the people were extremely proud of it and I remember the day we opened the hall – we just built it in twelve weeks and consider it a bit of a record - for us anyhow.

They chaired me up the street after I came out from mass that Sunday and the formal opening of the hall took place. (People carried Fr McDyer in a chair, something like carrying a Pope in Rome.)

From that experience, I knew that they were very enthusiastic about co-operation. Then when I began to wander into the development of industry and sent out the call again that we wanted share capital, yea, they did rally around and produced (not as much as was required) but by their own standards, they did put up quite a lot of money for the first two industries we started.

Then I began to see that in spite of all the co-operation, they had the notion that having subscribed money to it, the business was no longer their responsibility. They'd give money but not help. It was most noticeable when you would have an AGM. (An annual general meeting). You'd be very lucky to have fifteen people attending the annual general meeting, whereas there were hundreds that were involved as share holders around the place.

So, I began to realise then that we were only a co-operative in name but not in fact. The fault to a certain extent lies with myself, if I had to do it over again and I would do it all over again. If I had to do it all over again I'd try and play it in a different way. Now, I did the stimulating verbally, in the church, announcements, small school meetings, even kitchen meetings. But, I began to discover that the verbal relationship that I had with them was not quite getting through - they didn't realise properly, I think that they had *a revolution on their hands*.

Some of them naturally would be timorous that being a local person, just a native of county Donegal and not having any business acumen, that it would be unwise to pursue this through, moreover, I don't think they shared quite the ideals that I had. As a matter of fact, I am certain they didn't share the ideals that I had.

So from these few points you see the general co-operation of producing shares began to move away out of their minds as I went along because my ideal was to develop Glencolmcille to the end of the line.

Kevin O'Kelly:
Your idea was to develop a kind of Christian Communism?

Fr James Mc Dyer:
Oh, it was, it was very much!

Kevin O'Kelly:
The people didn't take to it?

Fr James Mc Dyer:
It would be too hard to say – there were none of them hostile to it, but they didn't quite get the message. Now, if I had to do it all over again and hopefully some younger priest will be trying this here there or anywhere else, in other countries or in Ireland.

If I had to do it all over again, instead of communicating by word – I communicate it by the written word, I found that lots of my talks were being misinterpreted somewhere or another.

Some people might deliberately misinterpret them, some people perhaps through no fault of their own. But if I were beginning again, yea, I would have a weekly bulletin, sending it to every house – we are doing this, we intend to do that and this is the way we intend to do it.

The written word stands.

Kevin O'Kelly:
Was it spiteful misinterpretation?

Fr James Mc Dyer:
Ah well, in any community you'll always get a small vocal minority. I would say deliberately misinterpret and cast cold water. You'll always get a few pundits in a pub who will pronounce doom on anything new that's started, particularly if it is started by a native. If I was a foreigner, a German or an American or anybody like that, the feeling is very widespread in rural Ireland that the stranger, the foreigner, what he starts must be good but the native no.

Kevin O'Kelly:
After all, in the end, in the heel of the hunt, Glencolmcille has over reached itself hasn't it?

Fr James Mc Dyer:
To a degree it has that's true.

Kevin O'Kelly:
The hotel will have to be sold?

Fr James Mc Dyer:
The selling of the hotel will not spell the doom in any way of the rest of the enterprises that we have started. But we'll sell the hotel and pay off our creditors and hopefully we might have a few pounds to spare.

Kevin O'Kelly:
You had in fact overreached yourselves!

Fr James Mc Dyer:
Yea, I think we had in our anxiety to get as many enterprises going as possible and in the new format of the co-operative that is seven of us originally. We had to buy all the money, we had to buy all the money for new enterprises, and it wasn't a shareholding operation at all.

Kevin O'Kelly:
Would you say that your experience says something about the quality of Irish life of Irish society?

Fr James Mc Dyer:
Oh I think so. Far be it for me to say anything against the people of Glencolmcille – they're very fine.

Kevin O'Kelly:
No! They're a product of the whole Irish social environment, north, south east and west - my Dublin environment, your Donegal environment, Cork, Mayo, Belfast?

Fr James Mc Dyer:
Two or three points strike me about our Irish people as a result of my experiences in Glencolmcille and opinions I got expressed in other parts of Ireland. Co-operation in the form that I was trying to initiate it – intensive co-operation is not on. After all, if we recall Caesar's Gallic wars which I read as a primer many years ago and the Gallic wars were the Gaelic wars and he picked them off one tribe after another. Whereas, if instead of warring against each other, they had coalesced, they would probably have sent Caesar back to Rome with a bloody nose. But he picked them off one by one throughout Europe. Now I think we Celts, I'm afraid that residue of individualism, or not intensive co-operation it still remains. Ah, that's one thought that I have.

Perhaps, I was driving too hard to turn the community into a family that was my ideal which I did not achieve, but, still and all they are a very identifiable, closely knit community – that is a fact not my doing.

Kevin O'Kelly:
Do you think they are any better off now?

Fr James Mc Dyer:
Oh, yes oh yea, definitely!

Kevin O'Kelly:
If you were going to start again, do you think that they would be any more ready. Have you converted any to the idea that it is possible to drag yourself up by your own bootstraps?

Fr James Mc Dyer:
Well I always divide any community whereas it's Glencolmcille or any other rural community into three parts; those who are active and sympathetic; those who are sympathetic but not active and those who are neither active nor sympathetic. Unfortunately, I'd say that in most communities, the third is in the majority – neither active nor sympathetic. Of course you could have a fourth section, those who are unsympathetic and active, ha! ha! I think we haven't had those in Glencolmcille. But the first one; active and sympathetic, they are very much in the minority in any rural community in Ireland.

Kevin O'Kelly:
So, if rural Ireland is to be rejuvenated, we thought the common market was going to do it, now it seems as if the Common Market is going to let rural Ireland down – so many people would say they're disillusioned with it anyway. How is it going to be rejuvenated, apparently not by Christian communalism, Christian socialism?

Fr James Mc Dyer:
Well, no, I think myself, this is my considered opinion. Whilst blaming myself for not doing the type of communication by the written word that I should have done – but an excuse for

myself I didn't have time. I was too active, by nature I'm an activist and to sit down and pen out a bulletin every week I just didn't have the time for it, but having said that I still believe most earnestly that a community properly stimulated can really improve their lot immensely. It's completely out of the question to ask any community in Ireland for one hundred percent co-operation. It's just not on; perhaps I was too much of an idealist – that was what I was driving for all the time, one hundred percent intensive co-operation. Let us work as one family that is McDyer idealism, but it doesn't work out.

I think the method that perforce we struck upon is the best one, that is, a small group of intensely interested and dedicated people who are prepared to give all their spare time to the development of the community and take the risks, the financial risks.

We have taken immense financial risks. Ok! One thing has gone sour on us but that doesn't mean we are beaten, we may be down for the moment but not out. So, that it can be done I don't think that by itself is the solution. I think the time will come when that small minority group of intensely interested and dedicated people will get old as I am getting old. What's going to happen after they go? That was my thinking two years ago when I was promoting the idea of begin to sell right now.

Sell the hotel, we're selling it at the moment – I think we'll not stop there, every way that we can liquidate our fixed assets, we'll start doing because my reasoning behind that, and I would hope that any other people listening to this and thinking of community development, what will happen after their day even if it is a co-operative. When the thing gets going, jobs are created, I think sell and create the fixed assets into money.

The jobs have been created, presumably whoever you sell to will keep the jobs going and they'll be more professional business people than we are. But then take all that money which we intend to do and create a Trust fund out of it for the community. The best legacy I or my two colleagues can leave to Glencolmcille is to create a Trust.

Sell gradually everything that we can sell and if it is something that we cannot sell like the Folk Museum, bind it into the Trust as well. We should be able to assemble, if we sell in the right market, we should be able from our different enterprises – we should be able to sell a fairly sizeable amount of money.

At one time there, our fixed assets were reckoned to be about a million pounds worth, probably even more than that. But when we have all our creditors paid off, it won't be a million pounds that will be left to us. Selling gradually in the right market at the right time, the fixed assets we have created – then converted into cash, invest it as cleverly as you can and create a development Trust for Glencolmcille.

That is our experience plus our forward thinking. I would like that the people who are interested in community development won't reach for the stars as we did and try to create a family out of a community because we failed to do that. And not even think of too much of co-operatives along traditional lines because having paid their share capital a lot of people lose interest.

No, I'm very convinced myself that a small dedicated group would create as many enterprises as possible and having got them going (acting as catalysts as we did), having got them going, liquidate then and create a Trust. The value about a Trust and I don't know the legal, all the legalities about it but the value of a Trust is that it is unbreakable, it's there in perpetuity and I'm dreaming up ideas when we start out Trust.

We may start it in the next year or so, what and how we will apply it to the best uses in Glencolmcille – you've got to think what will any community be like a hundred years from and the Trust will still be in existence? One of the things we were talking about before we got started on the radio, one of the things we were talking about was social welfare; well I would like the Trust to have a special lean towards social welfare.

Kevin O'Kelly:
The poor and the old?

Fr James Mc Dyer:
The poor and the old – to top up what they were getting, to top them up to the level of a non skilled worker. It would give them dignity and security – I'd like that, I'd also like that the Trust would apply itself to environmental protection too. But however, we're wandering very far perhaps, from the duties of a priest – I'm dreaming into the future now!

Kevin O'Kelly:
What you seem to be calling for the salvation of rural Ireland and perhaps the nation, in the tumultuous years that seem to be coming, is for disinterested entrepreneurship working within the capitalist system to make sense out of it for the local community and then opting out.

Fr James Mc Dyer:
That is quite right!

Kevin O'Kelly:
No, socialism though? Christians for socialisms, you've seem to have demonstrated to your own satisfaction that it doesn't work!

Fr James Mc Dyer:
I'm sorry to admit it but I think you are quite right. With intensive socialism with which I was aiming in Glencolmcille is not on. At one time though, mind you to be fair again to the people of Glencolmcille – this is all very small farm area, only about eight acres in every farm and poor land.

Now, when I was applying myself to the agricultural development of the place here, I persuaded one hundred and ten farmers to communise for an experimental ten years. But when I went to look for a loan or a grant for the operation – a loan I was looking for, none of the responsible authorities in Dublin would have nothing to do with it! It wasn't Christian, yea, ha! ha! So they told me anyhow and I walked out and banged the door. Ha-ha! But it was an intensely Christian idea because that was the high point where I was trying to get these hundred and ten to down fences and treat it as one farm for an experimental ten years. The way I was trying to sell it to them here is they would be one family, working together for one goal. And fair play to the people of Glencolmcille, I didn't want to take them all on, but a hundred and ten of them were agreeable to down fences for an experimental ten years.

Kevin O'Kelly:
That's the great might have been?

Fr James Mc Dyer:
That's the great might have been! And the tragedy of tragedies was that the responsible Departments hadn't the sagacity or the nerve to support that which was supported by some departments in Dublin. We would either have failed or we would have succeeded –if we had failed it wasn't a terrible loss, it was going to be experimental work but if we had succeeded as I'm fairly convinced we would then we had created a tremendous headline for the small farm areas of rural Ireland, right down the whole west coast. I really do believe it would have rolled, whereas as you know in the EEC the small farmer, the very small farmer hasn't a chance at all, not a chance!

Kevin O'Kelly:
Well now that you, as you say yourself, are retiring from the development scene ...

Fr James Mc Dyer:
Not quite yet!

Kevin O'Kelly:
Well not quite yet, you are thinking of doing it.

Fr James Mc Dyer:
Yea!

Kevin O'Kelly:
Are you retiring depressed because you'd seem to be justified in a certain modicum of depression because it just didn't work?

Fr James Mc Dyer:
Yes! Ah, slightly depressed but when I look back on all that we have achieved, yea I'm rejuvenated to a certain extent. I suppose I classify myself as an idealist and an activist and if ideals aren't achieved by an idealist, naturally he will suffer some depression and I have.

If anything had gone sour on us, at any time as has been done over the years I always did suffer intense mental strain and depression.

Kevin O'Kelly:
What would be the bright side? What would have been the good thing that came out of it? You look to me like a man that on the whole is content with the life he led?

Fr James Mc Dyer:
Well, from a religious point of view and I hope that the Almighty is listening to us, hah, hah, from a religious point of

view I felt that I was carrying out the work of a priest. Normally, a priest is not expected to embroil himself in business matters and I don't in any way claim to be a business man. I just wanted to get things started and hope that it would go from then on. But, from a Christian point of view, I think we have done a fairly good chore for the people of Glencolmcille.

They were in a very, very weak condition with massive emigration – no job opportunities, whatsoever and that has been completely turned around. In place of extreme pessimism which was abounding here, we have created a situation where there is great confidence instead of being ashamed to admit that they were from Glencolmcille – some of them have told me that they are proud to say they are from Glencolmcille.

That has been done, but I would like that the Almighty would take note of that I myself as a priest, in addition to the need to preach charity, charity and all the other virtues on a Sunday – I have gone out and did my best to implement these virtues in an active sort of way. And I have in addition to doing my normal duties as a priest in a spiritual sphere, I have extended that as many other priest have done, extended that, reaching my hand out to help people in a material way. In doing so I think I have been fulfilling the wishes of our Creator.

Kevin O'Kelly: Canon James McDyer,
who died in 1987,

Ar dheis Dé go raibh a h-anam

The Problem of the Small farm in the West of Ireland
Alan Bestic: The Importance of Being Irish,
by permission Orion Publishing Group

The official argument of course, is that the man's holding is too small to produce a living and that therefore he must be helped, just as an urban worker can draw assistance when he is out of a job. One answer to that argument has cropped into many minds, only to be left unspoken for reasons of expediency. It is simply this: add all the little uneconomic holdings together and make them into one big, viable holding.

The reason why this is not broadcast too loudly is suggested by John Healy, parliamentary Correspondent of the Irish Times. He wrote a book recently about his home town, Charlestown, in Co. Mayo, which is dying currently, like so many others; in it he said:

Today there are politicians in Leinster House, who see, as the solution for the West the creation of a dozen big communes on the Soviet style. The fear of political reprisals stops them from saying it aloud. But if they had an assurance that the first one would be opened by an Archbishop, sprinkling holy water on it, they would get courage and promote the idea.

There is however, one man who is not afraid to speak out on this explosive subject though, because of his job, he would seem to be in greater danger from reprisals than any politician. He is a priest, Father James Mc Dyer, one of the most remarkable people I met in all my travels around Ireland. His parish is Glencolmcille on Glen Bay in Donegal overlooking the Atlantic Ocean. It, like Charlestown, was dying: but Father McDyer has put a stop to all that nonsense, in the fourteen years he has been there. By co-operative effort, hard work and vision, he has stopped the emigration that had this hamlet down to 250 people, but raised the standard of living higher than it ever has been before.

It has been a big job; but then it was a big man I met in the Presbytery, a heap of a man, who walks tall. His voice has a slice of the north about it, soft, Donegal north; his label has a badge in it to say that he does not drink, though a bottle of whiskey is always kept handy for visitors; his eyes are keen with alert bewilderment and his talk is laced with an irony that never really wounds very much.

I asked him what he had been doing in Glencolmcille and why he had been doing it. He decided to take the second question first.

'Before I came here,' he said, 'I worked in London.

I met a lot of emigrants there, mostly from rural areas, and the sight of them made me feel a sort of shame that we had to depend on a country we had fought to absorb our redundant youth. We seemed to be getting our priorities wrong-talking about the past and doing nothing about the present - going on about self-discipline and efficiency being the price of freedom, but not paying the price.

'The first thing I did was to build a village hall. It was not the answer, of course not true progress, but I had to have a basis for financing my plans. It was not a parish hall, incidentally, but a people's hall, to use Maoist language. Every halfpenny we take there goes into the development of the community.

Then I started on social amenities – getting roads built, rehabilitating the school, chasing up people so we could have water, electricity, a dispensary. It all took time, though the local authority was very good about the roads and students from seven countries came through the World University service and helped us channel water to three-quarters of the houses.

'But why electricity?' I asked. 'I thought everyone could have electricity.'

'So they can,' he said. 'But some local people didn't want it here. They said it would be too dear and too dangerous. I had to sell them the idea and believe me, it was a hard sell because they were very conservative.'

He paused awhile; and then he went on: 'That's one of the troubles about the west. It was the progressive ones who left. Anyway, to get back, I knew roads and water and electric light weren't enough. None of it made sense as long as there were twenty-five young people leaving Glencolmcille each year. I knew I had to provide work, an incentive; and that was when I began to think of co-operatives.

'For years the politicians had been promising us a factory, but we'd never seen sight of it. However, I decided to have one more go and I wrote to Mr. de Valéra, who was Taoiseach – Prime Minister – at the time. Then just in case it got lost in the post, or something, I wrote to Mrs de Valéra.'

Father McDyer, to the amazement of his parishioners, got government help to start a factory. He chose a traditional occupation – weaving. A start had been made on what was to be a remarkable community enterprise.

'But I knew that it still wasn't enough,' he said. 'The land alone will never save Glencolmcille. Neither will a weaving factory. Not even together could they do it. What we needed was four or five pillars on which to build.'

Today he has them. There is his vegetable factory, in which they process their own vegetables in their own factory and sell them through Erin Foods, who gave them technical help and a guaranteed market.

Few people up here had heard of celery,' he said. The Department of Agriculture had heard of it, all right, but they said we wouldn't be able to grow it here. They spent a couple of hours pleading with me not to grow vegetables, saying it was too stormy, too dark, too everything. But I started and it grew beautifully. They suit the sort of pocket handkerchiefs of land we have here.'

Father McDyer has built his pillars and is building still. He has introduced progressive methods of sheep and pig farming. Glencolmcille has now three modern piggeries and five more are about to start. He is laying down a traditional pattern of farming where no tradition existed.

He has a textile co-operative that pays a dividend of seven and a half per cent to the workers and shareholders who own it. He has a metal craft co-operative, where a retired silversmith teaches young apprentices an ancient Irish craft. His food-processing factory employs ninety-five people at its busy times, enough to make many a foreign participator envious.

Most significant of all, however is his building co-operative. It has been a long time since Glencolmcille needed new houses. 'Youngsters are getting married.' He said. 'There weren't a whole lot of weddings when I came here, and, when they did wed; they were thirty to thirty-five years of age. Now they are coming along to me at the age of twenty-one or twenty-two. The co-op has built two houses already and is working on three more.

We're other plans too. We're thinking of going in for mushroom farming. I'm promised a market for it and it could be a very profitable farmyard enterprise. We may have a go at bees too. They could produce an extra £50 a year.

We're not a bit interested in an individual's earnings, you see; but we are intensely interested in the family earnings. One family here had a total income of £250 a few years back. Now they are earning together £1,300 and their farm is only six and a half acres. There are five in the family. One of the children emigrated a few years ago and another is studying at the technical school. They rear pigs and the wife is working in our knitting co-op, working at home. The other children are working in our factories. Our knitters can earn as much as five pounds a week. I went over to America on a cheap excursion flight and fixed up direct markets, cutting out the middleman and putting thirty per cent more profit into the pockets of the workers.

All this happened in the face of appalling apathy. Twenty per cent of the farms are held by ageing couples with emigrant families. Another twenty per cent belong to middle-aged or elderly bachelors.

Father McDyer told me: 'I would ten times prefer to face any Government Department in Dublin than to sell any idea locally. Straightaway, I can write off forty per cent of the people here as those who won't co-operate.

I suppose I could solve the whole problem by a stroke of a pen, by luring one big enterprise to run the lot. But I believe that God gave us land for a purpose; it is wrong to depopulate the land.

In the second place, I'm sufficient of a socialist to feel that it would not be fair to bring a big capitalist here to cream off the profit, pay the serfs and then, perhaps, at the first sign of recession, pull out, leaving everyone high and dry. To my way of thinking, all sources of wealth in Glencolmcille belong to the people of Glencolmcille; and the frontiers of the family are not the four walls of the house anymore, but the perimeter of the community in which they live.'

It was at this point that he mentioned something which I thought I would never hear from a priest in Ireland. He said: I must tell you about my commune....'

'It is true, of course, that the Christian Church operated communes long before Karl Marks was born and that the lives of monks and nuns are based on their community; but that, the conformists say, is different, or, as a rather superior English Jesuit put it: 'It's all right for us, but not for *them*!'

Father McDyer, however, is not a conformist. He told me: 'About two years ago, I decided to have a real go at this commune idea, though I must admit I didn't call it that. I used a nice, wee Irish word: meitheal, which means a group of people working agriculturally together for a common cause.'

'First I took some expert advice from the Agricultural Institute to keep me on the right lines. I showed them the plans and they gave them the green light, economically. After that I approached 130 local farmers and said: "Folks, how about knocking those fences down and working as one family? I guarantee three basics to every house: free turf for your fire; potatoes and milk; and work at standard agricultural rates for every able-bodied man in the community.'

'I explained to them that the fences would stay down for ten years to give the idea a chance and that the head man would be a technocrat, who would introduce the most modern farming methods for what would be, in fact a farm of 19,000 acres in mountain and lowland. Beneath him would be a committee of farmers, elected by themselves. After three years, I said, there would be full employment for women, too, under-roof farming around the farmhouse.'

'Do you know what? Out of the 130, 112 agreed to come in with me. It took them a bit of time to make up their minds, mind you, but in the end they signed on the dotted line.

After that I went straight to Dublin to talk it over with the Department of Agriculture and other officials. I wanted to borrow £124,000 – it works out at £6 an acre – to get the most modern equipment available for that farm. I told them that the loan would be repaid in ten years and thought they would be delighted with the idea.

But not on your life. A whole team of them spent hours trying to pick holes in my plans. When they couldn't do that, they said "Father, the whole idea is un-Christian; and you are hiding that under a cloak of piety.'

'Gentlemen,' I said, 'you are all experts in your respective fields; but you will have to admit that in this gathering I am the only expert on Christianity.'

Father McDyer returned to Glencolmcille deeply disappointed. He told me: 'I'm convinced it could have solved the problem of the small farms. I believe that the only solution for the West, in fact is voluntary collectivisation, even though some people still insist that it is a dirty word.

Even without his commune, however, he has transformed the bleak, beautiful hills that surround the hamlet of Glencolmcille, which has risen again. He has done something that nobody else, as far as I know, has been able to do in Ireland. So before I left, I asked him whether his methods could be applied to other parts of the country.

'If you searched all Ireland,' he told me, 'you couldn't find a tougher nut, geographically and psychologically, than Glencolmcille. If we can do it, anyone can do it. The time has come for the priest to become more involved in the worldly needs and aspirations of his people and temporally fill the vacuum of leadership, even though it meant sacrificing his leisure time. The best way to the soul is through the stomach, for it makes no sense to ask a couple if they've said their prayers, when they are worrying about the grocer's bill and what is happening to their daughter in Birmingham who has not written.' He smiled suddenly and said: 'I suppose you've heard they call me Stalin?'

'I'm ahead of you', Father,' I said. 'They've grown tired of that one. Now they are calling you a bit of a Hitler.'

That was true. I had had many talks in Dublin about Father McDyer before I headed for Donegal and too often the air had hung heavy with the cloying smell of faint praise, a poison that the Irish use with excruciating subtlety. I had kept plugging away, however, trying to discover whether there was one positive way in which his work could be faulted; and it was then that they began pinning unpleasant labels on him in the hope that somewhere a seed of doubt might be sown.

'A bit of a Hitler?' he said. 'That's a new one. Well, well ... what do you know!'

He was still smiling, as he stood in the presbytery door to wave me good-bye. I guess that he was thinking about his commune; and I made a bet with myself that the next time I passed through Glencolmcille, it would be there.

The attitude of the Establishment to co-operatives, let alone collectives, is distinctly cool; and I heard it suggested that once that official financial assistance for Father McDyer trickled through most reluctantly and in hope that he would fail and that the dangers of his wicked doctrine would be exposed. Nevertheless, co-operatives are bursting out all over, particularly in the fishing industry, which all of a sudden has begun to bustle.

Togra Taighde

Sa thogra thaighde seo pléifear an éifeacht a bhí ag an Athair Mhic Daidhir ar Ghleann Cholm Cille.

Owen Lyons, Letterkenny

(Printed here by courtesy of Owen Lyons)

Tá éifeacht an tAthair Mhic Daidhir ar Ghleann Cholm Cille fós le feiceáil fiche cuig bliain i ndiaidh a bháis. Idir na tionscnaimh thionsclaíochta, na tionscnaimh chúlturtha agus na tionscnaimh phobail a chur sé i bhfeidhm bhí an-rath aige agus é mar shagart cúnta, agus níos moille mar shagart paróiste Ghleann Cholm Cille. Tá sé d'aidhm agam san aiste seo:

- Plé a dhéanamh ar na heachtraí a chruthaigh agus a d'fhorbair meon an ghníomhaí shoisialaigh a bhí ag Mhic Daidhir.
- Déanfar comparáid agus codarsnacht idir an tAthair Mhic Daidhir agus Naomh Columba, beirt a raibh éifeacht mhór acu ar Ghleann Cholm Cille
- Cur síos a dhéanamh ar na heachtraí a spreag an fuinneamh a bhí aige nuair a tháinig sé go dtí Ghleann Cholm Cille ar dtús.
- Leargas a thabhairt ar stádas Ghleann Cholm Cille roimh theacht an tAthair Mhic Daidhir agus plé a dhéanamh ar an argóint nach raibh an ceantar chomh olc is bhí na meáin chumarsáide, chomh maith leis an tAthair Mhic Daidhir é féin, ag cur in iúl ag an am.
- Anailís a dhéanamh ar na tionscnaimh agus an ar an dóigh a chur sé bhfeidhm iad, ach le béim ar leith ar stádas na

dtionscnamh sa lá atá inniú ann, fiche cuig bliain i ndiaidh a bháis.

Déanfar é seo uilig thuas trí staidéar litríochta agus agallaimh a dhéanamh ar daoine ar nós Liam Ó Cuinneagáin atá mar stiúrthóir teanga Oideas Gael, údar 'The story of Fr McDyer of Glencolmcille: A Revolution on Their Hands' Liam McGinley agus daoine eile a bhí ceangailte agus atá ceangailte go fóill leis na tionscnaimh áirithe. Daoine ar nós Mary Anne Nic Giolla Easpaig, is ea an tAthair Mhic Daidhir a chur í i gceannas ar an chomharchumann cniotála agus Kathleen NicFhionnghaile, a bhí mar mhúinteoir scoile sa pharóiste i rith ama Mhic Daidhir. Tá taithí phearsanta agam féin ar chuid de na tionscnaimh a thosaigh an tAthair Mhic Daidhir, a dtig liom a úsaid chomh maith.

Na heachtraí a chruthaigh agus a d'fhorbair meon an ghníomhaí shoisialaigh an Athar Mhic Daidhir

Sa roinn seo déanfar plé ar na heachtraí a chruthaigh agus a d'fhorbair meon an ghniomhaí shoisialaigh an Athar Mhic Daidhir. Is é an creideamh, a thuismitheoirí, a chuid laochra agus Cogadh na Saoirse na rudaí is mo a d'fhorbair an meon seo agus le linn a óige. Dár leis an Athair Mhic Daidhir é féin is ó shaol an tí agus shaol an cheantair thart ort agus tú ag fás suas, is iad sin a chruthaíonn meon an duine agus iad fásta: *'I am quite sure that the earliest influences of home and environment deeply affect the character of the future citizen and man'* (Mc Dyer, 1982: 10). Ag glacadh leis an ráiteas seo tá go leor le feiceáil le linn a dhírbheathaisnéise a thaispeánann seo. Ag déanamh cur síos ar am dinnéir an Domhnaigh, nuair a bhíodh béile deas déanta ag a mháthair achan seachtain don teaghlach, dúirt an tAthair Mhic Daidhir go raibh a chuid tuismitheoirí i gconaí ag labhairt faoin deis nach raibh acu difear a dhéanamh den saol: *'time and time again we were reminded that our parents were in no position to leave a legacy behind them, but that they would try to give each of us a second-level education, and after that it would remain with ourselves to chart our own courses'* (McDyer, 1982: 13). Saol crua a bhí ann ag an am, bhí éifeacht an Ghorta Mhóir ann go fóill: *'The phenomenal upheaval of mass migration and mass death which resulted from the Great Famine altered Ireland's social structure profoundly'* (Quinn, 1999: 134). Chomh maith le seo bhí rudaí ag fáil níos measa mar gheall ar Chogadh na Saoirse, bhí a lán daoine ag dul ar imirce agus is é comóradh a chuirtear ar ócaid a bhíodh i dtigh an imircigh an oíche sular imíodh iad. Bhí éifeacht mhór ag na comóraidh sin ar an Athair Mhic Daidhir agus é óg: *'The most indelible impression of my childhood and adolesence was what was called in Donegal "the convoy" or comoradh'* (McDyer, 1982: 9). Beidh gráin an Athar Mhic Daidhir i dtaobh na himirce le feiceáil i rith an thogra seo.

Tionchar eile a bhí ar mheon an Athar Mhic Daidhir i dtaobh an ghniomhaí shoisialaigh nó na laochra a bhí aige. Is ón léitheoireacht a d'fhoghlaim sé faoi dhaoine ar nós Cú Chulainn, bhí a fhios aige cheana faoí Íosa Críost agus bhí éifeacht ag an Aifreann chomh maith le focail chliste a thuismitheoirí: *'Mass had the greatest influence on us all. It was the pervading deep conviction of our parents that we were on this world for a short time'* (McDyer, 1982: 13). Chomh maith le seo bhí Micheál Ó Coileáin go mór i súile na ndaoine ag an am agus é ag troid i gCogadh na Saoirse: *'these were my heroes, and I'm sure they exerted a powerful influence on my child mind, as I fretted over work that was planned for me, and I longed for the day when some kind of self-determination would be within my grasp'* (McDyer, 1982: 12). Ag fánacht le téama Mhicheál Ó Coileáin agus Chogadh na Saoirse bhí éifeacht mhór ag an stair agus go háirithe scéalta a Athar ar a mheon: *'our feelings also stemmed from the history we learned, and from the traditions handed down from father to son about the disgraceful treatment of our peoplr meted out by successive British governments'* (McDyer, 1982: 20) chomh maith leis a chuid taithí phearsanta féin: *'He remembers being bludgeoned by them as a child on his way home from mass'* (McGinley, 2007: 1). Mar gheall ar na heachtraí seo cruthaíodh meon láidir náisiúnachais ina intinn: *'It was this and the fact that he remembered the 1916 Rising as a six year old that gave him a strong patriotic streak and a strong desire to oppose oppression of all kinds, especially when it was against his people'* (McGinley, 2007: 1+2). Thosaigh sé ag smaoineamh faoi dhaoine na hÉireann, go háirithe nuair a scoilteadh an tír idir Phoblacht na hÉireann agus an Tuaisceart: *'I felt cheated then and I have felt cheated ever since. . . I resolved that if ever the opportunity arose I would work indefatigably for the good of our people'* (McDyer, 1982: 23). Mar gheall ar seo shocraigh air bheith ina shagart in áit doctúra ionas go mbeadh sé ábalta níos mo a dhéanamh don phobal: *'the priesthood offered me a permanent love of people and a love of work I would be required to do for them. . . in the context of fifty or sixty years ago , the only social worker I knew was the priest'* (McDyer, 1982: 27).

An tAthair Mhic Daidhir agus Naomh Columba: Comparáid agus codarsnacht

Déanfar comparáid agus codarsnacht idir an Athair Mhic Daidhir agus Naomh Columba sa roinn seo. Bhí sé mar aidhm agam agus mé ag déanamh taighde don thogra seo cur síos a dhéanamh ar an Athair Mhic Daidhir mar Naomh Columba nua do Ghleann Cholm Cille ach i rith an staidéir litríochta agus go háirithe i rith m'agallamh le Liam Ó Cuinneagáin chonaic mé nach raibh an smaoineamh seo inchréidte don chuid is mó. Duirt Liam Ó Cuinneagáin dom go raibh sé: 'deacair Mhic Daidhir a chur i gcomparáid le duine ar bith' agus gur: 'fear taistil a bhí ann', i gcodarsnacht leis an Athair Mhic Daidhir a d'fhan i bParóiste Ghleann Cholm Cille ó 1951 go lá a bháis.

Agus sin ráite, áfach, tá cosúlachtaí le feiceáil eatarthu, mar a dúirt Liam McGinley: *'St. Colmcille had brought the Christian faith to Glencolmcille; like Mc Dyer, he influenced greatly the lives of the people there'* (McGinley, 2007: 11). Bhí a fhios go maith ag an Athair Mhic Daidhir go raibh sé ag leanúint thuras Naomh Columba ó Thoraí go Gleann Cholm Cille agus duirt sé gur chinniúint a bhí ann: *'and it seemed to be my fate to retrace his footsteps for a place to which I was now assigned not only was evangelised by him, but actually bore his name. It was called Glencolumbkille'* (McDyer, 1982: 46). Dé réir mo chuid léitheoireachta thug mé faoi deara gur féidir módh bolscaireachta eile a bhí ar intinn Mhic Daidhir agus é ag déanamh comparáide idir é féin agus Naomh Columba. Cosúil leis an áibhéal a rinne sé ar dhrochíomha an Ghleanna ionas go bhfaighfidh sé aitheantas ón Rialtas d'úsaid sé an chomparáid idir é féin agus Naomh Columba chun smacht a chur ar na daoine trí eagla a chur orthu i bhfoirm mallachtaí: *'McDyer establishes himself on a verbal par with Colmcille, tactitly reminding the villagers that, like the saint, he too has the power to conjure social transformation via verbal utterences'* (Quinn, 1999: 147). Módh éifeachtach a bhí seo mar chréid na daoine ag an am go raibh cumhacht na mallachtaí ag na sagairt, nuair a chur me céist ar Liam Ó Cuinneagáin faoi dúirt sé: 'bhí scéalta mar sin ann, ar an dóigh sin thig leat a rá go raibh siad ag cur Mhic Daidhir i gcomparáid leis na seanfhilí, daoine speisialta a raibh ábalta mallacht a chur ar dhaoine nó mar sin dé'.

Ní sin a t-aon am a d'úsaid an tAthair Mhic Daidhir an chomparáid idir é féin agus Naomh Columba mar fhoirm bolscaireachta. I gcás cruinniú a bhí aige le státseirbhísigh ní raibh rudaí ag dul go maith dó agus chuir sé na státseirbhísigh i gcomparáid leis na druideanna a sheas in éadan Naomh Columba nuair a tháinig sé go dtí an Ghleann ar dtús: *'The druids have gone but they have left their peers behind in you boys, the senior civil servants. The modern druidical mist is your feasibility study'* (McDyer, 1982:67)

Na heachtraí a spreag an fuinneamh a bhí aige nuiar a tháinig sé go dtí Ghleann Cholm Cille ar dtús.

Tá cur síos déanta agam cheana ar na heachtraí a d'fhorbair meon an ghniomhaí shiosialagh a bhí ag an Athair Mhic Daidhir. Dá bhrí seo tá sé soiléir a fheiceáil nach raibh Oileán Thoraí oiriúnach don mhian a bhí aige daoine na hÉireann a chuidiú. Bhí sé i Sasana ar feadh deich mblian agus é: *'involved in one project after another'* (McDyer, 1982: 40).

Suaitheadh cultúir a bhí i gceist dó agus é ar Oileán Thoraí, ní raibh Gaeilge líofa aige agus dá bhrí seo bhí deacrachtaí aige leis an chumarsáid: *'McDyer describes himself as entering immediate culture shock by donning the role and the robe of a simple country priest'* (Quinn, 1999: 141). Fosta ní raibh morán le déanamh ann dó agus cibé iarracht a rinne sé tionscail a thosú ar an oileán theip air: *'He found the island very restrictive. . . He felt there was not enough work for him to do in Tory and tried in various ways to create work for himself. . . He attempted to set up a knitting industry to increase available money in the community and to reduce emigration but was not successful'* (Mac Cuinneagáin, 2002: 254). Dár le Liam McGinley ní raibh deis fhorbartha ar bith ar Oileán Thoraí mar gheall go raibh sé chomh imeallach sin agus go dtógfaidh sé i bhfád ró-fhada na hábhair a bhí i gceist foirgnimh a thógail a thabhairt anall ar na báid. Dár le Liam Ó Cuinneagáin: 'Bhí sé tar éis obair cruaidh a dhéanamh i Londáin i rith am an chogaidh ach silím, sagart óg, bhí a lan fuinnimh aige, ní raibh Toraigh dul a bheith deacair dó mar bhí sé og agus láidir ach bhris sé a chroí, níl aon cheist faoi sin, ní raibh sé ábalta imeacht ón áit. . . Sílim cosúil le morán daoine eile nach bhfaca sé todchaí don oileán'. Bhí a chuid frustrachais le feiceáil agus é ag imeacht ó Thoraí: *'The measure of my frustration can be judged by the precision with which I counted the length of my sojourn on Tory Island. It was four years, six months, and twelve days'* (McDyer, 1982: 41). Bhí sé ar a bhealach go Gleann Cholm Cille, ceantar nach raibh chomh difriúil ó Thoraigh ach: *'all that mattered to Fr Mc Dyer was that Glencolmcille was on the mainland'* (McGinley, 2007: 11). Bhí sé réidh chun a chuid fuinnimh agus a chuid dhiongbháilteachta a scoilteadh amach ar pharóiste Ghleann

Cholm Cille, spreagtha ó na heachtraí a d'fhorbair meon an ghníomhaí shiosialaigh ina intinn agus é óg, an náisiúnachas agus an imirice: *'A fierce resolve gripped my mind. . . Perhaps I was influenced by the traditional nationalism in which I was nurtured. But certainly I am sure that I was moved by the injustice that had been done to our people over the centuries. The tears that I witnessed in my youth, and which I now witnessed in Glencolumbkille, activated and solidified the determination in my heart'* (McDyer, 1982: 50).

Gleann Cholm Cille roimh Mhic Daidhir

Is é an cheist a dhéanfar pléigh ar sa pharagraf seo nó an raibh Gleann Cholm Cille chomh olc is a bhí na meáin chumarsáide, chomh maith leis an Athair Mhic Daidhir, ag cur in iúl ag an am? Tá sé ráite ag an Athair Mhic Daidhir é féin, sa leabhar 'Fr McDyer of Glencolumbkille' a dhírbheathaisnéis, agus é ag déanamh cur síos ar Ghleann Cholm Cille i dtearmaí tionsclaíochta, imirce agus talmhaíochta nuair a tháinig sé ann ar dtús: *'And here I saw it happening before my own eyes, for Glencolumbcille was dying – and the killer disease was emigration. There was no industry. . . no hope of prosperity for those who worked with the land. The vitality of the community was ebbing fast'* (McDyer, 1982: 49). Dé réir agallaimh le daoine áitiúla chomh maith le staidéar litríochta tá sé faighte amach agam nach n-aontaíonn na daoine leis an íomha bhriste ghruama seo a bhí an tAthair Mhic Daidhir a chur ar Ghleann Cholm Cille. San agallamh a rinne mé le Liam Ó Cuinneagáin dhearbhaigh sé dom go raibh na fadhbanna luaite agam thuas ann, ach nach raibh Gleann Cholm Cille níos measa ná áit ar bith eile sa tír ag an am: 'ní raibh na tithe go maith, ní raibh na bóithre go maith, ní raibh aon solas, bhí se olc agus duine ar bith a raibh airgead acu le himeacht, go Sasana nó go Meiriceá, fuair siad an ticéad agus d'imigh siad. Na daoine a bhí i Meiriceá bhí siadsan ag sabháil airgid chun chur na 'bhaile é sa doigh is a rachadh an chéad duine eile sa teaghlach anall chucu. . . ní raibh sé níos measa ná áit ar bith eile ach bhí sé olc'. Ní amháin go raibh an dearcadh ann nach raibh sé níos measa ná áit ar bith eile ag an am (Liam Ó Cuinneagáin thuas) ach dár le fear amháin a bhí mar bhall de phobal Ghleann Cholm Cille a scríobh litir chuig eagarthóir 'The Irish Times', a d'usaid Eileen Moore Quinn mar pháirt den mhiontráchtas a scríobh sí, bhí stádas Ghleann Cholm Cille níos fearr ná formhór na gceantracha Gaeltachta in Éirinn ag an am: *'when he (McDyer) came, he found a parish that was far above the average. . . in the West in terms of industry and sophistication –ours was one of the parishes in which the traditional crafts of weaving, handknitting and embroidery still flourished. . . We were not the broken, apathetic people projected by the media'* (Quinn, 1999: 157).

I rith m'agallaimh le Liam McGinley thuig me cén fath a raibh an tAthair Mhic Daidhir ag cur drochíomha ar Ghleann Cholm Cille. Dhearbhaigh sé domh go raibh: 'go leor daoine nach raibh ró-shásta leis an tAthair Mhic Daihir ag ráit go raibh Gleann Cholm Cille in ísle brí' ,ach bhí plean aige. Dár le Liam mcGinley is é a rud a bhí sé a dhéanamh nó iarracht: 'an smaoineamh a chur amach go raibh cuidiú de dhith ag Gleann Cholm Cille ón Rialtas agus is é an t-aon dóigh a bhí sé ábalta é seo a dhéanamh nó trí áibhéal a dhéanamh ar droch-íomha an Ghleann'. Módh bolscaireachta a bhí ann. Tá sé ráite ag Liam Mcginley Chomh maith is é an fath nach raibh daoine ró-shásta faoin drochíomha seo nó mar níor inis an tAthair Mhic Daidhir an plean do formhór na ndaoine, ach amháin na daoine a raibh cóngarach dó. Bhí a fhios i gcónaí ag an Athair Mhic Daidhir go raibh tábhacht mhór ag baint leis na ceird áitiúla: *'It has long been said, rightly or wrongly, that the women of Donegal by their diligence in producing such Home-Crafts as knitting crochet and embroidery, have kept our economy from total collapse'* (Mc Dyer, 1970) agus bhí sé chun iad a úsaid mar bhuntaiste dó féin agus don phobal agus é ag iarraidh tionscail a thosú sa Ghleann.

Ná tionscnaimh – Cád futhú anois?

Sa roinn seo déanfar anailís ar na tionscnaimh a thosaigh an tAthair Mhic Daidhir i bParóiste Ghleann Cholm Cille. Déanfar cur síos gearr ar an dóigh a chur sé na tionscnaimh i bhfeidhm ach beidh béim ar leith ar stádas na dtionscnaimh sa lá atá inniú ann, fiche cuig bliain ó a bháis. Déanfaidh mé iarrachtcloí leis an ord inar bunaíodh na tionscnaimh ó 1953 ar aghaidh.

Is é Halla Muire an chéad tionscnamh a rinne Mhic Daidhir. Tógadh é taobh istigh de thrí mhí sa bhliain 1953: *'The hall was formally opened exactly twelve weeks after it had begun'* (McDyer, 1982: 55). Ionad gnóthach a bhí ann ón tús, mar a dúirt Liam Ó Cuinneagáin sa leabhar cómoraidh caoga bliain: 'nach raibh aon oíche nach raibh rud éigin ar siúl'. Scríobh na daoine aistí ag déanamh cur síos ar Halla Muire agus na cuimhní a bhí acu air i rith na mblianta. Bhí na aistí seo bailithe don leabhar *'Halla Muire: Caoga bliain ag fás'*. Duirt an tAthair Séan. S. Ó Dubhthaigh, sagart cúnta ag an am, sa leabhar: 'is cúis áthais agus bhróid dúinn go bhfuil sé mar chroílár imeachtaí na h-áite go fóill'. I rith na mblianta tháinig athraithe ar Halla Muire, roimh foilsíodh an leabhar cómoraidh bhí an halla i rith athchóirithe, tógadh seomra ranga agus tá sé in úsaid sa lá atá inniú ann do Naíonra: 'Tá seomra aerach gleoite ag na páistí beaga atá ag freastal ar na Naíonra' (McGinley, E. 2003 *Halla Muire: Caoga bliain ag fás'*).chomh maith le seo bíonn biongó ann gach seachtain agus dráma bliantiúil. Bhí mé féin i láthair ag na drámaí seo agus tá siad go hiontach.

Is é an Taispeántas Talmhaíochta an chéad tionscnamh eile a thosaigh an tAthair Mhic Daidhir. Tosaíodh é sa bhliain 1954 agus bhí an-rath aige leis sna céad trí bliana. Bhí Éamonn de Bhailéara ann leis an seó a oscailt agus dúirt sé: *'If only rural Ireland could see this, then all would be well'* (McDyer, 1982: 63). Nuair a bhí rudaí ag dul go maith agus bhí clú agus cáil ar Thaispeántas Talmhaíochta Ghleann Cholm Cille ar fud na tíre mar cheann de na taispeántais is fearr i gCuige Uladh: *'At its peak, the exhibition featured over 1,600 entries in various categories, second in Ulster only to the Balmoral Show in Belfast'* (Donegal Democrat, 9/2/2010). Ach ansin tógadh an cinneadh chun deireadh a cur leis an seó: *'we considered that the show had done its work and we closed it down, Wisdom comes with experience, and often since I have regretted the decision'* (McDyer, 1982: 63). Ach sa lá atá inniú ann tá athbheochan tagtha ar Thaispeántas Talmhaíochta Ghleann Cholm Cille. Thosaigh sé arís sa bhliain 2010 agus tá sé ag dul ó neart go neart achan bhliain ó shin: *'We are delighted to be part of Féile Ghleann Cholm Cille, one of the most successful community festivals in Donegal every year,"* said Micheal

O'Gara, chairman of Taispentais Talmhaochta Ghleann Cholm Cille." (Donegal Democrat, 9/2/2010).

In ainneoin na deacrachtaí a bhí ag Earagail Éisc Teo nuair a d'oscail an mhonarcha sa bhliain 1962 agus sna blianta a lean na hoscailte, deacrachtaí talmhaíochta agus an athrú ó mhonarcha glasraí go monarcha próiseala éisc: ' Cé gur éirigh leo ar dtús ní raibh muintir an cheantair ag fás go leor glasraí. . . cuireadh tús le Earagail Éisc Teo.' (Ó Baoighill, 2000: 25) tá Earagail Éisc Teo. ag éirigh go maith sa lá ata inniú ann, bhain sé an duais: 'Seafood Exporter of the Year Award hosted by the Irish Exporters Association' (McGinley, 2007: 85) sa bhliain 2005 agus i dtearmaí airgeadais: *'The companies turn-over is in the order of 23 million euro plus'* (McGinley, 2007: 85). Dar le Pádraig Ó Baoighill a scríobh an leabhar *'Ó Ghleann go Fánaid'* : 'Dá mbeadh an tAthair Mac Duibhir thart bheadh bród air gur chuidigh sé pobal tuaithe a choinneáil beo, fostaíocht bhuan a chur ar fáil díofa, agus brí agus anam a chur ar ais sa cheantar'. Caithfidh mé féin buíochas a thabhairt dó fosta mar bhím féin fostaithe ag Earagail Éisc Teo le linn an tsamhraidh agus tá súil agam go mbeidh an samhradh seo chomh maith.

Sa bhliain 1966 tosaíodh an mhonarcha chniotála sa seanscoil agus chuir an tAthair Mhic Daidhir Mary Anne Nic Giolla Easpaig i gceannas: *'knowing her worth as a manageress. . . the presence of the vacant school. . in 1966, the year the factory was opened'* (McDyer, 1982: 83). I rith m'agallamh le Mary Anne nic Giolla Easpaig duirt sí liom agus í ag déanamh cur síos ar an rath agus na deacrachtaí a bhí ag an mhonarcha: 'bhí sé deacair ar dtús ach ansin bhí sé ceart go leor ar feadh tamaill, ach ní raibh na daoine ag obair ann óg, bhí siad ag fáil níos sine agus bhí éifeacht ag seo ar an mhonarcha, chaill muid daoine le pósadh nó le báis agus ní raibh muid brabúsach níos mó, ní raibh an margadh ann. Thosaigh an mhonarcha ag éirigh níos laige thart feadh 1979/80, druideadh an mhonarcha i mí Aibreain 1980 silím'.

Sa bhliain 1967 cuireadh tús leis An Clachán (Folk Village). Dár le Liam Ó Cuinneagáin spreagadh turas a thug an tAthair Mhic Daidhir go Daonpháirc Bun Raite smaoineamh An Clachán, mar a dúirt sé sa tráchtas a scríobh sé: *'Bunratty Folk Park probably inspired Fr McDyer to build the Folk Village Museum in 1967'* (Ó Cuinneagáin, 2010: 10). Nuair a bhí An Clachán idir lámha insítear scéalta faoin dóigh a bhfuair an tAthair Mhic Daidhir na lámhdhéantúsáin a bhí de dhíth fá choinne na seantithe sa Clachán; *'He would come into our homes and see something that he liked. . . He'd say, "I'll take that". . . and whatever it was, it was gone'* (Quinn, 1999: 154). Ach i rith m'agallaimh le Kathleen Nic Fhionnghaile d'inis sí dom: 'muna tógadh na sean-pots agus pans bheadh siad caillte anois ar scor ar bith'. Tionscnamh an-rathúil atá sa Clachán: *'It has thrived, being perhaps the most popular tourist attraction in the area'* (Ó Cuinneagáin, 2002: 260). Sa lá atá inniú ann bíonn thart feadh 40,000 daoine ann gach bliain dár le leabhar Pádraig Ó Baoighill agus tráchtas Liam Ó Cuinneagáin.

Tionscnamh eile a thosaigh an tAthair Mhic Daidhir nó an scoil fidil, nó Seachtain na bhfidiléirí a chuirtear uirthi sa lá atá inniú ann. Is seachtain í seo fá choinne fidiléirí de ghach aois, bíonn ranganna ann ón Luan go dtí an Aoine i Halla Muire, an bunscoil agus Oideas Gael. Bíonn an tseachtain seo ann sa chéad seachtain de mhí Lúnasa go bliantúil agus bhí mé féin ar pháirt den scoil ar feadh trí no ceithre bliana agus mé níos óige.

Le é Oideas Gael tionscnamh a thosaigh Liam Ó Cuinneagáin agus Seosamh Waston sa bhliain 1984. Bhí éifeacht mhór ag an Athair Mhic Daidir ar Liam Ó Cuinneagáin agus é ina fhear óg: *'Liam Ó Cuinneagáin, who was influenced greatly by Fr Mc Dyer as a young man'* (McGinley, 2007: 97). B'fheidir gur spreagadh an éifeacht seo Oideas Gael. Chuir mé céist ar Liam i rith m'agallaimh leis an mbeadh Oideas Gael ann gan an tAthair Mhic Daidhir: 'Bheadh Oideas Gael ann, bhí muidinne chun Oideas Gael a dhéanamh ar aon chuma ach thug sé an-thacaíocht duinn'. Sa lá atá inniú ann tá Oideas Gael an-rathúil. Bíonn daoine as tíortha ar fud an domhain ann i rith an tsamhraidh chun an Ghaeilge a fhoghlaim.

I rith an thogra thaighde seo d'fhoghlaim mé go leor faoi éifeacht an Athar Mhic Daidhir ar Ghleann Cholm Cille. Rinne mé cur síos ar na heactraí a d'fhorbair meon an ghníomhaí shoisialaigh agus chonaic mé go raibh éifeacht mhór ag a chuid tuismitheoirí, an creideamh, a chuid laochraí agus cogadh na saoirse ar mheon an Athar Mhic Daidhir. Mar gheall ar na éifeachtaí seo bhí sé ag iarraidh daoine a chuidiú, daoine na hÉireann ach go háirithe. Rinne sé seo i nGleann Cholm Cille, áit a d'úsaid sé modh bolscaireachta chun cuidiú ón Rialtas a fáil don áit. Chomh maith le seo d'úsaid sé an chomparáid idir é féin agus Naomh Columba chun na daoine a spreagadh chun tacaíochta a thabhairt do na tionscnaimh a thosaigh sé, nó a bhí sé chun tosachta. Dá bhrí na heachtraí seo a d'fhorbair meon an ghníomahí shoisialaigh a bhí ann thosaigh sé go leor tionscnaimh a bhí go hiontach don cheantar. Mar a thaispeáin mé san aiste tá cuid acu fós ag déanamh go maith agus tá siad iontach tábhachta don áit, i dtearmaí fostíochta go háirithe. Le héifeacht an Athar Mhic Daidhir ar Ghleann Cholm Cille a chur i gcúpla focail críochnóidh mé an aiste seo le focail an tAthair Mhic Daidhir é féin: *'Glencolumbkille was being bled to death by emigration, and underdevelopment; it is now on its feet as a viable community, combining small farming, industry based on local materials, and tourism'* (McDyer, 1982: 115).

Leabharliosta

McDyer, J. 1982. *Fr McDyer of Glencolumbkille.* Dingle, Co.Kerry, Ireland: Brandon Book Publishers.

Quinn, M E. 1999. *"Nostalgia is our future"*: Self-Representational Genres and Cultural Revivial in Ireland

McGinley, L. 2007. *The Story Of Fr.McDyer Of Glencolmcille: A Revolution on Their Hands.*

McDyer, Rev. J. 1970. *West Donegal Resource Survey: An appraisal by Rev. J. McDyer*

Mac Cuinneagáin, C. 2002. *Glencolmcille: A Parish History.* Dublin 2: Four Masters Press

Halla Muire: Caoga bliain ag fás. 2003. Coiste Cuimhneachain Halla Muire.

Donegal Democrat 9/2/2010 (http://www.donegaldemocrat.ie/news/local/revival_of_glenc olmcille_agricultural_show_1_2001885)

Ó Baoighill, P. 2000. *Gaeltacht Thír Chonall: Ó Ghleann go Fánaid*. Binn Éadair, BÁC 13, Coiscéim.

Ó Cuinneagáin, L. 2010. *Fr. McDyer – a pioneering champion of community development*. Cumann Thír Chonaill i mBaile Átha Cliath.

Agallaimh

Liam Ó Cuinneagáin (stiúrthóir teanga Oideas Gael)

Liam Mcginley (údar *The story of Fr McDyer of Glencolmcille: A Revolution on Their Hands*)

Mary Anne Nic Giolla Easpaig (bainisteoir an comhurcann cniotáil idir 1964 agus c. 1980)

Kathleen Nic Fhionnghaile (muinteoir scoile sa pharóiste i rith am Mhic Daidhir)

Printed in Great Britain
by Amazon